centigrad

robert calvert

Typeset by Jonathan Downes,
Cover photography: John Hughes - with thanks
Layout by SPiderKaT for CFZ Communications
Using Microsoft Word 2000, Microsoft Publisher 2000, Adobe Photoshop CS.

First published by Quasar Books 1977
Second edition by Voiceprint 2007
This edition published in Great Britain by Gonzo Multimedia

c/o Brooks City,
6th Floor New Baltic House
65 Fenchurch Street,
London EC3M 4BE
Fax: +44 (0)191 5121104
Tel: +44 (0) 191 5849144
International Numbers:
Germany: Freephone 08000 825 699
USA: Freephone 18666 747 289

© Gonzo Multimedia MMXII

ISBN: 978-1-908728-07-4

centigrade 232

FROM THE ORIGINAL EDITION:

ROBERT CALVERT was born in Pretoria, South Africa in 1944, but moved to England at the age of two. He went to school in London and Margate, and later studied building technology at Canterbury Tech.

Always interested in the literary arts, he began writing and performing poetry around 1967, and in that year formed a street theatre group in London's Chalk Farm, called 'Street Dada Nihilismus'. Shortly afterwards he met up with Britain's premier space-rock band, Hawkwind, with whom he has now evolved from resident poet into lead singer. He co-composed the band's hit single, *Silver Machine*, and directed their unforgettable *Space Ritual* stage show, appearing as poet and narrator. As well as recording with Hawkwind, he has also made two solo albums, *Captain Lockheed and the Starfighters* and *Lucky Leif and the Longships*.

More recently he has turned his wide talents to the theatre, *Stars that Play with Laughing Sam's Dice,* his play about Jimi Hendrix, was staged by the Pentameters Theatre in 1976, and he has since written a full-length stage play scheduled for production in the Spring of 1976.

CENTIGRADE 232 is Robert Calvert's first collection of poems. He is currently at work on yet another new departure – a science fiction novel and ideas for further stage plays and poetry collections.

DEDICATION
This book is for Kay, Paulyn, (Alexander, Helen and Daren), Jarmilla, Elly, Sandy and Jude.

introduction

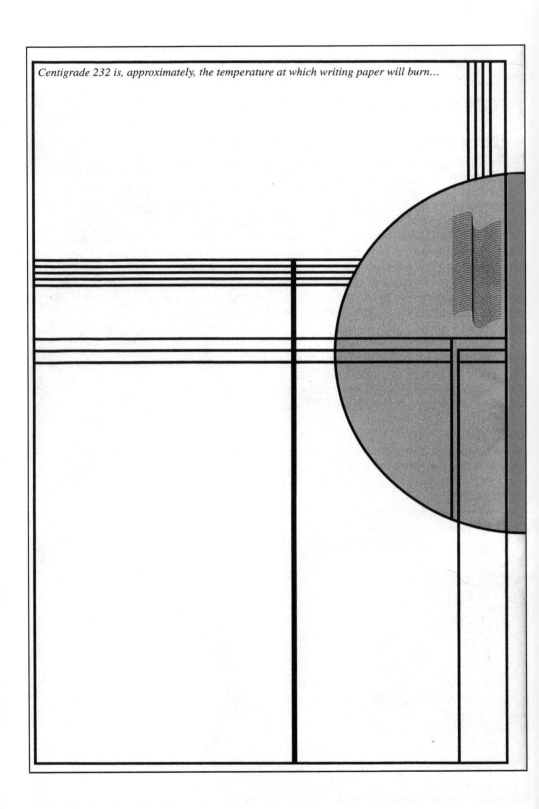

Centigrade 232 is, approximately, the temperature at which writing paper will burn...

Contents

Nail-Biter
Mountaineering in Suburbia
The Last Kitten
Caterpillar
Snowfall
Insomnia
Storm
Overslept
The Day We Hunted Birdsong
Fountains in the Park
Coots

RAGWORM IN A ROCK POOL

Shell
Beach Combing
Ragworm in a Rock Pool
Seagulls (for Richard Bach) (1)
Seagulls (for Richard Bach) (2)
Recollections of a Seaside Love Affair
The Drowned Man

THE RED BARON REGRETS

Churchill's Secret Rock Deal
The Red Baron Regrets
John Keats of Margate
Voodoo Child (In Memory of Jimi Hendrix)
The Legend of Esra Pound

the first landing on medusa

SWING

Holding off invasions is quite hard work
for one small boy. Now it is time
to play. To take the short-cut to the park
where swings hang from their scaffold frame

like rows of empty perches in a cage.
And bird-like, with his arms upraised,
he holds, for a moment, the launching stage.
Then goes. Feet first. Upwards. Is poised

for a long split-second among the leaves
and clouds. Then falling from the sky
flies backwards, and the playground's asphalt heaves
beneath him like a switched back sea.

It rocks the heavens, this clanking machine:
an engine to swing a planet
through its axis, made simply out of chain
and wood, with a child to man it.

ODE TO A CRYSTAL SET

There wasn't much to you at all: a pair
of earphones, and a dial to twiddle:
but you beat the sixgun and the saddle,
you were futuristic as Colonel Dare.

And so was I, in your bakelite 'phones,
tuned-in to the insect lecture of morse,
always at war with the alien force
of crackling static's interference zones.

And at night I could hear weird language drone
with your dark conches pressed against my ears,
and dream there were voices among the stars.
The secret of knowing was mine alone.

With your earthed antenna divining air,
you traced the future of your tran-sisters.
Oracular coil, you were the cat's whiskers
till I heard the superhetrodyne's blare.

THE FIRST LANDING ON MEDUSA

I'd rather the fire-storms of atmospheres
than this cruel descent from a hundred years
of dream, into the starkness of the capsule.
Two of our crew still lay suspended, cool
in their tombs of sleep. The nagging choirs
of memory, the lengths of tube, and wires
worming from their flesh to machinery,
I would have to cut. Such midwifery
is just one function of the leader here:
floating in a sac of fluid dark, a clear
century of space away from Earth.
One man stared from the trauma of this birth,
attentive to the tapes assuring him
this was reality, however grim;
our journey's end. The landing itself
was nothing. We just touched upon a shelf
of rock selected by the Automind.
And left a galaxy of dreams behind.

Full waking took us days to realise.
Adjusting to the newness of our eyes
we stayed inside, performing simple tasks.
Hardly speaking, faces set like masks.
until the time came round for us to set
the first feet on this world, to get
our samples, and erect the instruments.

A barren planet, but to all intents
another Eden opening its gates
for this chosen few who'd outslept the fates.
Anonymous, identical, in our suits
we entered the air-lock. My weighted boots
would be the first to touch this unknown stone.
I led some distance, then I felt alone.
So I turned. And saw that the others were
standing still. I radioed to make them stir.
But got no answer. So I waved my arm.
But they still stood as though a stoning charm
had taken hold. I made my slow way back
and found each man was frozen in his track.
I hammered my gloved fist on visor-plate
and pulled at pressure-padded arms. A state
of utter trance had overtaken all my men.

My mouth felt dry. My fingers stiff. And then ...

ODE TO A TIME FLOWER

*As he carried the flower back on to the terrace, it
began to sparkle and deliquesce, the light trapped
within the core at last released......*

*Raising his head, Axel peered over the wall again.
Only the farthest rim of the horizon was lit by the
sun, and the great throng, which before had stretched
almost a quarter of the way across the plain, had now
receded to the horizon, the entire concourse abruptly
flung back in a reversal of time, and appeared to be
stationary.*

Your calyx hides a nectary of time
that with my fingers I could pluck as easily
as sounding strings to recite their chime,
and your most exquisite petals melt icily
in my palm. To hold the flow of moments past
as carefully as I would my last
few seconds left on Earth. Would that be crime?
Or if I picked you just to see you turn
to crystalled pearl in my eyes and learn
how man is Angel on his way from slime.

Did heedless Eve think twice before she broke
the enjewelled fruit from its brittle stem?
Or the first man to reach out and stroke
the marijuana leaf, condemn
himself for greed when harvesting
and burning such a golden thing.
As this dreaming poet who just then spoke
of your sacredness, and is now prepared
to do exactly as he first declared
and make of his useful words a joke.

But not quite as easy after all
I find, as my fingers reach to grasp,
your gleaming head to wrench from its tall
transparent stalk, they refuse to clasp.
As did Pandora's eager hands hold still
at the thought of the box containing ill.
Or the stoned explorers of Medusa stall
for time not entered in their log
before they dared the petrific fog
that holds them still in its timeless thrall.

... ... a nectary of time
that with my fingers I could pluck as easily
as sounding strings to recite their chime,
and your most exquisite petals melt icily
in my palm. To hold the flow of moments past
as carefully as I would my last
few seconds left on Earth. Would that be crime?
Or if I picked you just to see you turn
to crystalled pearl in my eyes and learn
how man is Angel on his way from slime ...

SOME SKETCHES OF A HAND

1. Outstretched like this the palm
does not give much away
to one unversed in palmistry.
It could just as easily
slap a face as receive a gift.

It was a hand, much the same
as this, that spun the first wheel.

2. Solid, compact, as good
for propping
as for uppercutting chins:
it was a fist, similar to this,
that upheld the first thinker's head.

3. This opposing tackle is the secret
of the hand, its key. That makes
it possible to grip. Depress
a hypodermic's valve.
Hitch a lift. Flick pages.
Signify that all is well.

It was a thumb like this
sent Christians to the lions.

4. This index could be pointing
to your guilt, or the way
to the public lavatories.
A finger such as this
could pull a trigger
or pick a nose.

5. For a creature that only has one head
one pair of hands seems quite enough.

THE STARFARER'S DESPATCH

I would have liked you
to have been deep-
frozen too, and waiting
still as fresh in your flesh
for my return.
But your father refused,
to sign the forms,
to freeze you.
Let's see, you'd be, what,
about sixty now. And long
dead by the time I get
back to Earth. My time
suspended dreams were full
of you as you were when I left.
Still under age.
Your android replica
is playing up again.
It's no joke.
When she comes
she moans
another's name.

SONG OF THE GREMLIN

I focused the magnifying glass
that brought the downfall of Icarus.
Balloons were easy; a simple pin.
Or a knife in the case of the Zeppelin.
That blade was the cause of many a prang
in the early days of stick and string.
I am the gremlin. I was there.
Making mischief in the air.
And always will be, wherever man
flies in the face of Creation's plan.

THE PAUSE

When the stillness
of the beginning
was shattered
by the word
A fragment of it
fell to the earth.
It tried to make
a home for itself
but could find
no resting place
for long. It stumbled
at the roots
of a liar's tongue
but was soon
spat out. It lived
for an instant
in a murderer's hand.
It lingered
at the fingertips
of a thief.
For a time it hung
at the edge of war
by clinging
to a shrub of peace
which soon gave way.
A politician juggled it
so much in his speech
that it fell, almost
senseless, to the ground.
Later, a small boy
who was about
to stamp on an ant
got it stuck
to his shoe, and had
a moments trouble
in shaking it free.

THE CLONE'S POEM

I am a clone.
I am not alone.
Every fibre of my flesh and bone
is identical to the others'.
Everything I say is in the same tone
As my test-tube brothers'
voice.
There is little choice
between us.
If you had ever seen us
you would rejoice
in your uniqueness
and consider every weakness
something special of your own.
Being a clone
I have no flaws
to identify.
Even this doggerel that pours
from my pen
has just been written by
another twenty telepathic men.
Word for word.
O for the wings of any bird
other than a battery hen.

CENTIGRADE 232

At Lexington they are going to burn
a hoard of books for charity.
Round these towering volumes the flames will churn
as night and winter's dark they spurn
and threaten with their clarity.
The fire's fierce theatre draws herds of folk
all willing to be hypnotised;
anemones of flame and reefs of smoke
enchant us so, we'd gladly choke
to see the dark so well disguised.
"Oh look, the Bible's all on fire", we cheered
at its catching. "Oh watch it flare".
It was like this of old, when witches reared
against the stake; we stood and peered
at such Aladdin caves of air.
These mushrooming billows of coral form
the fevered brain of fire on high,
whose dream of destroying the world by storm
will, in the ashes, still be warm
long after its illusions die.

FAHRENHEIT 451

Some notes; whole pages
of scrawl, and crossings out;
dud lines that never would
quite reach
the flash-point of a poem;
for these I sat up half the night.
I stand them in a tin
and set the match.
Time is worth much more
than paper
but seldom burns
with such bright flames
as these failed drafts.

THE NAKED AND TRANSPARENT MAN
GIVES THANKS

Amid the folding of all greenness left
I give my thanks, whole-heartedly for life
for this vermilion tapestry, warp and weft
of the blood-vein's fabric. Its threads are rife
conspicuous; easy-meat for knife
or microbe, and the many ills that kill.
And yet are stubborn and abundant still,
with ruins of ages around me, strewn
like wreckage of an unsuccessful probe
among the craters of a wasted moon.
I extend my thanks for this living robe
and its pulsing weave, to the moth-holed globe
and unravelling, almost threadbare sky
of the failing sun under which I lie.

buster keaton and the virgin sperm dancer

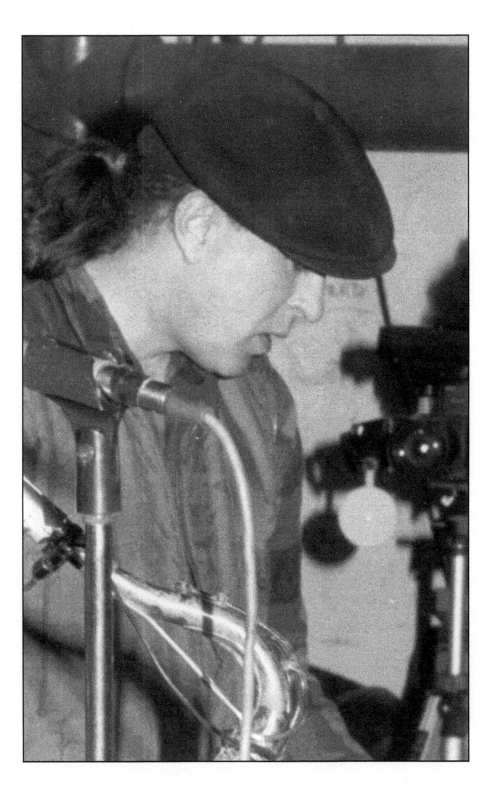

DANCE STEPS

I.

The music plays horizon and sky,
while your partner stands erect
extending branches in all directions.
Then you take up your position.
Drifting above her, like a cloud.
When the music plays warm air you rise,
condense in the coldness,
and turn to rain.
With this your partner starts
to put out leaves.
And when all the leaves have grown
your head looks down
while your body descends
to walk giraffe-like around the tree.
Then you, at the end of your stretched out neck,
begin to eat the leaves.

2.

You are the swimmer.
Your arms plunge and curve
with the grace of dolphins.
Your partner is the shore.
Playing the seas between you
is the music and its silence.
Your partner is an island
that sways with trees.
She is where the earth
has forced its way above the sea.
You swim.
And you continue swimming,
with her swaying,
until, at last, you fall
exhausted into each other's arms.

3.
You are storm,
an invasion of gale
and flailing rain.
Your partner is a room.
A shuddering bubble
of calm that bursts
free and floats
to take its place
as moon.
The music plays
the taste of electricity
while you fork out
phosphorescence
and the crash of blackness.
She rides the storm.
The circle of her yawn
widening
until it has become
a giant tea-cup.

LINES FOR A CONCEPTION CARD

The moon blacked out; a perfect night.
A flight of Wellington set course
for Bremen. Two uniforms
were discarded in a hotel room.
On one side she lay reading
while his cigarette burned down like a fuse.
The last night of their leave.
Mars was in ascendance.
All this was before you were thought of.
His hand reached for the switch
and plunged the room into falling dark.
The bomb doors opened.
The child-making moment flared.
And buildings smouldered.

LADY WITH A LOOKING GLASS

She casts her eyes,
like pebbles,
into the pool
of the mirror`s stillness
and stares and stares
at the rippling image,
until her gazing trails
like a net
to haul the illusion
of her looks. She looks
out of the mirror
at herself looking in.
And catches little wriggling smiles
then releases them
to the silver of freedom.

THE SIREN

I was never really one
who was moved by music
to much of an extent.
But when I heard
that song, that song
that played on the strings of the wind,
I could not resist. And half my crew
were sirenized so out of mind
we lost our course, went
aground on rocks, and wrecked
beyond repair.
Now I've heard her singing
closer to,
without the orchestra of storm
and the swaying choir of waves
for backing, it is nothing
very special. Not much
of a tune to it. Nothing
to really knock you out.
And as I plot
my position, escaping
on trades of ink into maps,
I can see the flashing of her eyes
at the edge of my sight.
Like the knife-
glint glances that stab
from doorways in the red-
light districts of any port.

BUSTER KEATON AND
THE VIRGIN SPERM DANCER

To get to her door
they have to scale
tall buildings, swing
from flag-poles,
swim canals.
When they finally arrive they find
his white face has dissolved.
She looks for her key,
her smile still intact.
It is a blue door.
They climb the stairs.
He keeps failing backwards,
doing somersaults
for her amusement.
There is nothing to say so he says
nothing, nothing. His chair
collapses. She curls up
with laughter,
the rough serge of his suit
prickles his skin.
Nothing that he does makes any noise.
He watches her dance
in the flickering quiet
discarding clothes.
Then he climbs into bed,
in night-cap and gown,
and wastes his breath on a candle's flame
that refuses to be blown out.
While she rolls, all night,
in the stunt-man's arms.

YOUR TIME

When it is your time
there is no heat between us
as there is with hounds and bitches.
We are far too tame.
We let our breeding screen us
from what it is that itches
and no longer has a name.
When it is your time
the light stays on for longer
while we catch up on our reading.
I lie, with my tome,
coiled near you like a conger.
While secretly you're bleeding.
The clock is a metronome.
When it is your time
your touch can blast a vineyard.
Fade purple cloth. Evacuate
bee hives. In your term
you can calm the seas. Safe-guard
from boils, barrenness. I wait.
Less conger, more wrinkled worm.

A REFUSAL TO MOURN THE REMOVAL,
BY SURGERY, OF TWO BENIGN TUMOURS

No, I will not think of you
laid out under lamps: the glare
of eyes, above white bandit-
masks, all trained on you; your flesh
cut back and held by clamps, while
instruments investigate;

your pale, blue-veined breasts both touched
with expert vermilion
openings, like two lip-sticked
mouths, smiling, one on either
side, a vision of Magritte's.
I will think of something else

and smoke a continuous
cigarette. I will only
think of the surgeon's pencil-
marks, you wore the night before,
as a fading endorsement,
for a readmission to some

orgy, a eunuch doorman
applied to your breasts as you
stepped outside to take the air.
I refuse to think of you
asleep beneath the breathing
mask of a black Ganesha:

your trunk sucking oxygen;
your eyes gone in; under more
dazzle than this scarred page's
angle-poise. I will not mourn
your imagined death, for the taste
of tears. I will only think

of the morning, when I'll come
with grapes and flowers to rouse
you from your anaesthetic
shell; to unwrap and open
the shy kiss I shall give you;
when you lie in albumen-coloured sheets.

As exquisite as though you were newly hatched.

CIRCLE LINE

Seeing that I still had eight more stops
to go, and had already read
the maps and advertisements from end to end,
and studied my own double-
eyed, four-eye-browed freak
of a reflected face for far too long; I took
to noticing another. Through a kind

of snooker-shot of glances
aimed against the glass, I could see her
staring; but could not be sure
if it was at me. I smiled,
and saw her turn to speak
to someone next to her. I also turned:
and unexpectedly our eyes engaged

for just the instant that it takes for looks
to rocket through the tunnels
of an unguarded gaze, and arrive
at the real self. Badly shaken
with embarrassment, we both looked back
at our images: safely imprisoned
in the hurtling stillness of the glass.

AN UNPOSTED LETTER

Four pages, folded and enclosed
in an envelope of stone.
It lies and smoulders like a meteor
on my desk. The globe revolves;
the sextant drills for directions;
the telescope is focused for your home.

Four thin slices of forest
inscribed with fossilized hieroglyphics;
a packet of desert seeds,
it has been lying there for days.

It was pain to write. It was rivet
of plate on plate of meaning.
It was blinding steel sparks
of the pain from which it came.
I wore my deception like a welding mask.

To say what there will be
no need to have said.
To say only my need to say that there was
a need to say that there was
no need to have said.

A migrating flock of stamps
has invaded my room.
Letterboxes snarl as I pass.
The envelope is swelling.
Already the desk has collapsed
beneath its weight.
The instruments are smashed.
The surrounding houses
are being evacuated.

the urban
mountaineer

THE CLERK

From nine in the morning
until five in the evening
he worked in the office:
sat at a desk with a telephone,
a typewriter, and a bottle of pills.
When the telephone rang
it meant that he had
to pick up the receiver and say hello.
When the typewriter rang
it meant that he had to shift
its carriage from the left to the right.
When his head rang
it meant that he had to take a pill.

One day he found
that owing to a fault
in the ventilation system
the only intake of air
for the whole department
was through a hole in his desk.
He toyed with this for a while,
placing his Roget's Thesaurus over the hole,
observing, with pleasure,
the effects of air-withdrawal
on the rest of the staff.
(Their faces turning faintly blue).

And not being one to miss a trick
next morning he turned up for work
with a wad of chewing gum
and an aqualung in his briefcase.

CLEANING A RAPIDOGRAPH

There is nothing more obstinate than this
prima donna of precision pens.
Neglect it for a while and it will hiss
at your attempts to make amends

by scratching at the page without a sign
of the eloquent arias of its line.

Take it to the nearest sink, unscrew,
and let its pent-up blackness flood:
a sudden massing of all you drew;
a burst of murdered dragon's blood.

Watch, as it merges with the water: plumes
of squid's secretion; of octopus fumes.

In a while of soaking, the hollow nib
should free itself of clotted ink.
And reassembled, be just as glib
and nimble as the speed you think.

It took me less that a minute-and-a-half
to write this, with my Rapidograph.

LETTER OF COMPLAINT
TO THE COUNCIL

The sky is coming in through the roof.
The melted sun is dripping
its golden oils on our clean white cloth.
Aeroplanes, like dead flies,
are floating in our soup.
There is no waiter to complain to.

Our dining table is cluttered up
with scraps of cloud
and Dutchmen's trousers.
At night, the stars descend
like flakes of dandruff around my head.
While I am trying to roll the perfect cigarette

I have to dodge the tumbling, planets.
We have placed a bucket, strategically,
to catch the moon. Our carpet is ruined
by the yolk of broken galaxies
and trodden Zeppelins.
This morning, while waiting yet again

for the man to come and fix the hole
I noticed also that a blade
of wilderness has forced its way
through a crack in the floor;
there are grains of desert
in the living room ......

FLY ON THE SCREEN

One of those tiny ones they use
in experiments
that live their life-span out in three
minutes, I believe.
It was almost invisible
as it crawled among
the Saigon refugees; became
a mole on the news-
reader's cheek.

Instead of killing, I tried to
flick it gently from
the screen. But it kept on coming
back for more cathode-
rays, as though their bombardment gave
it powers. Traversing
smoke-filled skies, and war-torn borders;
the landscape of a
talking head.

In spite of all its minute size
I found it hard to
concentrate on the images
this indifferent black
dot occupied, made mockery
of. The picket-lines
at the factory gates it dwarfed;
the football crowds it
trampled on.

It was making headline news, this
fly. Interrupting
every scene with a flash of wings.
Like one of those long-
running, political scandals
that take up most of
The News At Ten, until they "die".
I looked at my watch.
Not long now ....

Its three minutes would soon be up.

THE RECOVERY

Waking this morning
I found I could breathe
fresh air again,
the protoplasmic swamp
in which I'd sunk
had disappeared
as suddenly as a bubble,
and I could smell
the scents that had been absent
in the seven days or more of my cold:
when I lay shipwrecked in a flood
of whale sperm,
and the rhinovirus trumpeted.

With tissues piling up around me,
like the failed drafts of a fevered poet,
I forgot the smells of food,
and took my meals as coldly
as one swallows Pills. And flowers
were just for looking at.
But now, with my newly hollowed nose,
I go about the house
unstopping bottles of cologne
and aftershave; sniffing,
like a connoisseur, the rich bouquet
of perfumed soap and lavender,
tins of tobacco, and instant coffee jars

When a cure
for the common cold is found:
they'll have to invent
another cure for complacency.

NAIL-BITER

To see the sufferer at work
on what's left of his nails, gnawing
as intently as some starved wreck
at a rat's bone, is harrowing

but rare. The act is somehow kept
a guarded secret, even from
himself; almost as though he slept,
or had blacked-out, while murder came

strangling out of his finger-tips.
But all the evidence is there
in these ten crescent-ended stumps,
like nails that might be used to claw

engravings in a prison's walls:
their edges frayed and worn away;
like broken off and blunted bills
of ten caged, vicious, birds of prey.

It may well be this habit saves
nothing but the need for filing.
But watch the teeth peel off the shives:
the lips are drawn back, are smiling.

MOUNTAINEERING IN SUBURBIA

From having made a thorough search
of handbag, pockets, wallet and purse,
we faced the fact that we
had lost the key to our room.
I said it would be an easy matter for me
to climb across from the bathroom and in
to our room. Only a distance
of two or three feet. But she
was not too keen on my going out there.
I opened the bathroom window, sensing the walls
and garden stiffen as I dipped
a cautious foot into the sky.
At sixty feet above the ground
you have only to step
on the upturned rake-head of the air
for its handle of concrete paving to come
flailing upwards to crack your skull.
(I knew in the glossy laurel bush
A weasel curved, with blood in its fur).
But I'd already launched myself
out of the safe square of the window frame.
I bridged my body, flung my legs out, clung
for dear life (scraping my shoes against the bricks)
and then, with one last effort, hauled
my sprawling selves from the void
of falling, and in to the room.

THE LAST KITTEN

Suddenly it disturbs a cool
and collected pool with its paw
for a mirage of fish
A Christmas gift for a child:
furry, beside itself with quiet,
the kitten catches imaginary things

in its growing claws. In play
its pink tongue tastes
and knows the flow of killings.
The scooped ears raised
like radar, scanning
the corners of the sky, and the long

grass, clear, at the core of its brand-
new mind. An enemy of birds,
it is fledged for quick flights
close to the earth. Already a killer
of mice in its stalking thoughts.
These milk-vicious teeth can nip

huge illusions of flesh from your proffered
finger. From pulling at a dead
shoe it spins to face the flying
things that flit, split-secondly,
from the walls. Attacks, and they vanish.
It licks its fur for blood, instinctively.

Has yet a system of ritual
moans to learn from itself;
to snipe at the night's quiet
with its ricocheting cries.
The mother, heavy with milk
and tired of this world, made old

by roofs and creeping Toms
(Straggled from fights:
lop-eared-torn-coats) watches
through yellow eyes slashed black.
Her last kitten. Hunched,
her shoulder bones the stumps of wings.

CATERPILLAR

Going out of the house I saw
the caterpillar stuck to a wall
it was green, and had tiny trees
of hair along its back.
When I returned it was still there,
the children agreed they wanted it
so I took a jar and held it like a mouth
to catch this falling morsel I had tipped
from its grip with the lid.

I dropped some leaves inside and gave
it holes for air. It lay
in a cataleptic trance, wound
like a snake-stone around itself.
Coming back from the dead, it first
extended itself for a leaf
of its cryptic shade, and clung to this
I held it up for the children to see:
a maggot at the core of a big glass fruit.

Soon it left the leaf and pumped
itself towards the walls of the jar.
On rows of prehistoric feet it flowed
against the glass, then curved
backwards in a graceful arc,
and with the rhythms of a cobra
attuned to inaudible flutes, it swayed
from side to side in search of space.
"It is a snake", my small son observed.

Fearing that its food would dry
and leave the creature parched
in some Autumnal desert, I let
some drops of water fall into its world.
Bored with its slowness, the children
went back to their toys.
When I next examined the jar
I found it had hung itself from the lid
like a living pendulum to gather time

about itself and form a chrysalis
where, mummified, the butterfly
would a wait its after-life:
suspended in a tomb of glass.
Next day my wife, while dusting
things about the house, accidentally
overturned the jar. The caterpillar
dell from its hold and struggled drunkenly
in a pool from which it could not be saved.

And not long after must have drowned
in the soak. For it did not curl up
as it does in faking, but lay stiff
in real death among the scattered leaves.
I washed the jar and its contents
out into the sink, and saw its body
spin for an instant in the plug-hole's whirl
before it was swept away
to the underworld of the drains.

SNOWFALL

The bloated sky has burst at last
and now the air is teeming
with these Arctic spores. They waste
no time. By early morning
they'll have grown a new world
to explore. Craterless, still gleaming

from creation's mint. An undefiled Planet.
Until the houses loom
like some invading fleet of brick-walled

space-craft, come to stake its claim.

INSOMNIA

I must have accidentally
tripped the switch
that turns the stillness on.

STORM

This house
is washed up
on a mountain
of rain.

The night
has made us
famous.
All around

huge microphones
are being tested
and flash-bulbs
blind our windows.

OVERSLEPT

On waking up I found
that kids from the school
across the road, had dragged
my bedroom into their playground.

Encircling, scribbling
with their brittle voices,
until the teacher's whistle blew
them up, like a hand-grenade.

Pelmets need putting up
Milk bottles washing,
Pictures to be hung.
Getting up is difficult.

If I were any God-like Kafka
I'd have my hero bristling legs,
But consider this state of indolence
Metamorphosis enough.

My beard crackles like earphones
against the sheets. The clock
releases a swarm of ticks.
Boiling kettles scream like mortar shells.

THE DAY WE HUNTED BIRDSONG

Where he'd got it I didn't ask,
I was so knocked-out to see it.
Double-barrelled, loaded with risk;
a real shot-gun. "Shall we try it?"

Humpo said, his screwed-up lenses
X-raying me for cowardice.
Humpo lived for taking chances.
Keep away, was my mum's advice.

I followed him to Romney marsh.
The gun was in a fishing-case
tied to his cross-bar. "What's the rush?
I yelled, legs aching, "S'not a race".

We hid our bikes in leaves and went
on foot till we found clearing.
"Bet you've never been on a hunt,"
he said, in his voice for lying.

I watched him open up the case
The same cold way he gutted fish,
or fingered girls. He held the prize
of dented metal threat to flesh;

I looked after the cartridges,
while he broke the barrel to load.
Thick sedge thrived along the edges
of the lake. And the birds sang loud.

Then, without warning, Humpo fired
both barrels off. "C'mon. let's get!"
I croaked in panic. "No-one heard".
said Humpo, "don't be such a pratt".

He froze, one finger raised for hush.
Tilted eyes gone strangely vacant;
a snap-shot trapped by Agfa flash.
"Hear the birds? " he whispered, "I can't".

FOUNTAINS IN THE PARK

These fabulous statues,
that speak an everlasting,
cascading word;
that declaim an endless torrent.
of parabolic utterance;
that spout
without regard:
are blind and deaf
and ever in mid-speech.

COOTS

Where the sky has softly collapsed and floats
like a sail capsized in the green
of the drifting pond, a family of coots
continues feeding; while mallards preen

and dabble the sun. Close to the edges
where its food is massed and simple
to reach, an old coot dives for the wadges
of plant its young must have ample

supplies of for life. They squeak like squeezed toys,
bobbing helplessly in the wake
of the latest dive to escape the noise
and fetch the stuff to stuff its beak.

The body is a feathered bulb of black,
from which the shiny pate protrudes
as tiny as a turnip's crest. Its neck
is perpetually craned for weeds.

The mallard's an aristocratic fop:
exotic, painted, on parade.
While coots are drab workers who never stop
feeding their grey, demanding brood.

If the dandy mallard had had this fate
he'd be just as bald, and daft, as a coot.

ragworm in a rockpool

SHELL

Years we spent
Living in a coiled shell
Only just
Out of reach of the tides.
We were afraid of going out
In case of crabs,
Whose eight-legged scraping kept
Us awake at night.
There were always
The gliding cries of the sea
And the threat of gulls
So we kept inside.
Where the sea's depth
Echoed relentlessly.
Our children thrived
On plankton, and kelp
Was always in good supply.
We drew them pictures
Of the outside world
On the floor of sand.
We never spoke of swimming.
We dazzled them
With sketches of the sun.
Years we spent
Living in a coiled shell
Waiting for the tidal wave
To come.

BEACH COMBING

My small son, unsure of his feet,
tottered beside me, shuddering
the world with his tiny boots;
my great strides jangled the stars
like fairy lights, as we walked to the beach:

To search the tide's edge
where the sea delivered
its rolled horizons and dissolving skies.
We prised the sun from its pebble of cloud
And watched it scuttle sideways out,
As we looked for sand seeds
To grow a desert in our window box.

RAGWORM IN A ROCK POOL

In this green, submarine
tundra of weed, the gigantic ragworm
drags its lengths of dragon blue
on monstrous millions of legs that cause
chaotic falls of sand; and the crystal sky
to oscillate. It lumbers by, like some
hand-painted, *papier-mâché* dinosaur
in a pouring carnival of freaks.
A crab's machinery has seized with sand.
Its shell feeds rust.
Ragworms sculpt
the fallen chalk.
They stitch the beach.
Are quick with sting.
An edible leviathan, writhing
for its stranded meal of green:
its brightly blooded bulk invades the air
as it hauls itself to feed. Until,
exhausted by the elements, and heavily
engrained with sand, it lies
among the mildewed weed; guzzling
like a living hose of slime.

SEAGULLS
(For Richard Bach)

(1)

These are the earliest birds to be heard
with their yelling hunger among the rocks.
Before the chorus of the dawn has stirred
they are wheeling above the sea in flocks,
already delving for their daily food.
They catch the worm that lesser birds exclude.
Gulls have no song. Their voice is only spurred
to shrieks, by greed or rage. A dumb gull locks
its wings and glides with legs absurd
and dangling, like the hands of broken clocks.

The most vicious creature found on this shore
has the power of flight. It has been known
for nesting gulls to swoop and go straight for
the eyes of unsuspecting dogs. Full grown,
a seagull's as big as the lizard-bird
whose some shrill threat of yells can still be heard
by man, when attempting to explore
the forsaken rocks it would seem they own
in the early light; when not quite so sure
of himself, he walks the furrowed beach, alone.

SEAGULLS

(2)

In the snow the seagulls
came to scavenge
scraps of bread
from the block shed roof.
The only birds that are visible
from my glaring window
are these airborne scarecrows,
sparrows' terror, they come
from the sea; with their bodies made
from jelly fish; beaks
from driftwood; wings
from cuttle-bone;
and their dangling feet
that are made from frogs' legs
painted red.

RECOLLECTIONS OF A
SEASIDE LOVE AFFAIR

Now, I am almost sure
it was the cliffs themselves
my love was deepest for.
As my memory delves
I find that there is more

of the touch of night-sand,
cold against my fingers,
than the feel of your hand.
And the voice that lingers
is of the sea. I stand

at recollection's edge
and vaguely gaze at white
inclines of face. I dredge
for sunken gems, and sight
the rock pool's lens and pledge

my words to them, not eyes
so long forgotten now.
I watched the sun's gold rise
with you but was somehow
more lover of the skies,

of spray and waves, more true
to them than I could be
to the pale ghost of you.
Our love was all at sea;
lost to the cliff-top's view.

THE DROWNED MAN

It must have been at some time in the night,
While the wild, loosened sky hung slack and flapped
Against our windows like a flag,
That this unknown sailor was drowning out
At sea. In surging cold: eyes bulged, mouth gaped,
Guzzling ocean to the last dreg.
While we slept easy, floating in our breath,
He still tossed and turned against the leaden
Dread that was weighing down his will,
Till bursting up for the third time his faith
Must have given way, and left this sodden
Wreck of flesh at rest in the squall
Of gulls the ruined sky of the morning brought.
Washed up from our pale dreams we lay still steeped
In our own warmth, could hardly drag
Ourselves from the tide's edge of sleep and out
Into the world: where we kept our heads, we hoped,
Above water; but felt its tug.

the red baron regrets

CHURCHILL'S SECRET ROCK DEAL
(based on a headline in *The Times*)

Whatever you do, don't
mention politics, said his manager.
Show them how you can twitch your jowls.
Make a V sign like you just don't care.
O.K.?
O.K.

They sat and listened
to the tapes in the A& R department's
quadrophonic office.
No-one looked
at anyone. They tapped their feet, and watched
the spools of the Revox
turn.

I like that track
about fighting
on the beaches,
said the man
from promotion.
Reminds me of *Blood,*
Sweat, and Tears.
I think we should
have a lyric sheet.

He did the cover
design himself,
his manager said.
It's a landscape
in Morocco...

Ah.

Well, we'd rather
have a photograph
of him in the homburg
and crombie, with a big
cigar. That's the image
we're going for.

O.K.?

O.K.?

O.K.

And we'd like to put.
Never Before in the Field
of Human Conflict out
as a single,
if you'll do
the remix we suggest.

Right?

Right.

Right.

Then why don't we
go down to the rail-
way carriage
and sign
the contract?

It's a pleasure to do
business with you
Mr. Hitler.

THE RED BARON REGRETS

*In the late afternoon of 22nd April (1918) Manfred
Von Richthofen was buried with full military honours
at Bertangles. Six R.A.F officers carried the plain
wooden coffin shoulder high from the hangar where
it had remained during the night, to the hearse, a
Crossley tender, and then the cortege moved slowly
away, preceded by a firing party of Australian
airmen and followed by more than a hundred Allied
mourners.*

(John Killen: *The Luftwaffe - A History*).

It is best, if this poem
is to be read aloud,
that it is read
by a chorus of voices
in accordance with Brecht
and his theory that heroes
should not be singled out
for praise.

I whole-heartedly agree
with that literary ace.

There is nothing very noble
in knocking another Icarus
out of the sky.
Snarling dogs scrapping
in some midge-ridden alley
have far more grace
than two squat planes
out for each other's blood.

It was not for the enemy's benefit
that I chose red,

instead of camouflage,
for my flying colours.
It was more so my own,
over-anxious men
would not accidentally shoot me down
in their haste to score.
And it wasn't only from superstition
that I told the press

I wanted no photographs
next to the plane;

but all the same,
some keen young cub
appeared from nowhere
and fixed me in his sights
as I climbed aboard.
I took off with my eyes
star-blind from flash,
and knew that mission would be my last.

I find it hard to fully understand
how I am carried to my grave

by men whose lives
I hunted for.
Whose fellows
I guided into fire.
They stand there,
Silent.
Their caps in hand.
Salute the empty sky with guns.

JOHN KEATS AT MARGATE

I became not over capable in my upper stories,
and set off pell mell for Margate, at least 150 miles
- because forsooth I fancied that I should like my old
lodging here, and could contrive to do without trees.

(Letter to Leigh Hunt, 10th May 1817).

I.
As he left the station
and entered the town
he felt there was something
missing about the place
but he could not quite...

The sky was in eclipse
with the sea, and waves of shadow
froze on the land. The silence
was so highly pitched
it made the eardrums ring.

There were no trees.

2.
Some children laughed
at him as he passed. Pointing
at his strange clothes
and hair. He poked

his tongue at them.
It was green,
veined and fringed
at the edges

Like a leaf.
3.
A word that Keats
had whispered to himself
flew from his piercing lips
and fell, like a spiked mine,
to the glass-like
surface of the sea.
Leaving a crack
with branches that reached
for the heart of shadows.
4.
After his tenth replay
on the pin-ball machines
he got bored with scoring
and tried the fruit-machines instead.
He hit the Jackpot
immediately, and won

an avalanche of acorns.
5.
He carved his name
on the leg of a giant
gull. And watched it fly
towards the west

with a forest in its beak.

VOODOO CHILD
(In memory of Jimi Hendrix)

With quicksilver fingers,
with kinetic fingers,
with incendiary fingertips,
he detonated the volcanic outburst of pandemonium
and loosened the torrent of sonic subversion,
with a guitar of riot and uproar,
with a furious, devouring guitar,
he wailed the disintegration of ecstasy,
he moaned the convulsions of the mind.
With a mouth of stereo ventriloquism,
with a drastic mouth of fire,
he howled the displosion of ascendant havoc,
he chanted the erupting sacrifice of ears.
With a mouth of lingual cunning
ejaculating tongues of surgent flame
he yelled the orgasmic atom's canticle.
He screeched the cataclysmic cries of gravity.
He split the drumskin dungeon of silence
and set its demon prisoner free.
Truly he sang the body electric.

the legend of ezra pound

ezra pound was a wild man from idaho who rode
through kensington on a high horse dressed
in fringed skins toting sixguns of lyricism
and a quick draw line of chat he rode right through
the doors of the cafe royal and blasted wyndham lewis
six times through the head to music of hysterical laughter
from the assembled wits

the barrelorgans of favourite verse stopped rolling
and their attendant monkeys covered up their eyes
and ears and chattering mouths of idiot drivel as lewis rose
to his feet exposing his forehead flowing with perfect
chinese characters of blood and the scars in his neck
where hemingway had hooked him with his whaling hooks
(and said look i have hooked the nastiest man in the
world) stood out like egyptian hieroglyphs

ezra moved with his magnetic beard into a bedsitting room
where he sat playing an enormous machine with keys and a bell
that made a sound like a horse-drawn fire engine over cobblestones
and released little flocks of images into the air that flew
out of the window and settled on passing bowler hats and made
them look like flowerpots or like black lampshades that hid
the brilliance of incandescent heads

one day t s elliot came by for tea and brought with him
a gigantic manuscript conveyed in bales on the heads
of native porters which he said was the wasteland and pound
took down a cavalry sword from the wall and a shotgun loaded
with blue graphite and later he handed mr elliot a handful
of pages and said this is all you need and from the rest
of the pages he made a flight of little suicide planes

ezra went to italy where he took up marching exercises
learning how to bring his iambic feet up higher than his head
until he found he could outbox *earnest* hemingway with just
his jackboots mussolini gave him a job as a disc jockey
but he never gave himself enough time to play any records
he was too involved in talking about his economic theories
that would save the world

the american forces network came for him in the night
to arrest him for offences against the air and they locked
him an iron cage where blackmen pelted him with peanuts
screaming fascist and experimental psychologists trained
stroboscopes on his dreams until he swallowed himself feet first
and turned himself insideout so no-one else could hear him speak
the doctors took twelve years to unravel him the right way
round and he spent the rest of his life in his daughter's
castle in spain striding the long stone corridors at night
reciting shadows and firing at the echoes of the past
with his guns of silence

Some of these poems have previously appeared in: *New Worlds Science Fiction Quarterly*; *Frendz*; *White Trash*; *The Purple Hours* (Tynecon anthology); *Pentameters Anthology*; *Oyster*, *Science Fiction Monthly*.

Recorded on: *Captain Lockheed and the Starfighters* (United Artists) *The Space Ritual: Hawkwind Alive in Liverpool* (United Artists) *Quark, Strangeness and Charm* (Charisma) and have been read on: Granada Television, Capital Radio and Radio London.

The poem 'Circle Line' was awarded first prize in Capital Radio's London poetry competition in May 1975.

First published by Quasar Books 1977, from which the introduction and dedication are reproduced.

Lightning Source UK Ltd.
Milton Keynes UK
UKHW01f0629180918
329097UK00006B/665/P